REFLECTIONS OF A HIGH SCHOOL GIRL

POEMS ABOUT LIFE, LOVE AND HOPE

KRITIKA PRAMOD KULSHRESTHA

THANK YOU!

I don't remember when I started writing poems. As a kid I hated essay writing in school. I found writing troublesome, but my mother made sure I turned in a decent essay every time. She'd spend hours editing and re-editing my work and wouldn't let me give up without figuring out how to help me write a good introduction to my essay. If I'm a writer today, it's because of the sheer hard work she put into my school essays.

Poems, on the other hand, seemed to be more free-flowing. I could play with their structure, and they didn't always have to rhyme. They were just expressions of my feelings, a way to pen my observations. There were no barriers I had to break down to write a poem. And that's how I fell in love with poetry.

I wrote for school competitions, got my poetry published in school magazines and each time I saw my published piece I was overjoyed. It filled me with a sense of pride. I even wrote poetry as farewell gifts for my friends.

I never imagined I'd end up enjoying a fulfilling career in writing and marketing, and I have only my foray into poetry to thank.

I began writing the first poem of this collection when I was in middle school then high school (as the title of this book suggests). Over the years, my life has seen some incredible highs and lows as I've explored different corners of the world, my eyes filled with dreams and my heart full of hope. Yes, it has been a long journey, and it's time these poems see the light of day. They've been waiting behind the curtains, and it's time I share them with you.

I'm thankful to my parents: my mother who single-handedly raised me after I lost my dad at the age of 17 and my dad who made me who I am even though some parts of my childhood and teenage years have faded away.

This book is for my mentors, my friends, my family, my favorite communities, and all the people who took a chance on me each time I tried to push the envelope, each time I tried to leap out of my comfort zone, and each time I had self-doubts about what I was doing. You've taken a chance on me and made a real difference in how my life has turned out. Without all of you, this collection of poems would not have been possible. This book is a way of expressing my gratitude.

If you've interacted with me in any way—on social media or in real life—you've added a dose of magic and inspiration to my life.

Thank you one and all! *Reflections of a High School Girl* is here, and it's yours. :)

Cheers,

Kritika Pramod Kulshrestha (not a high school girl anymore!)

Contents

1. Life is a Rat Race

It's a cold Monday morning,
and I'm still snoring,
the birds are chirping,
and the sky seems dark and hazy

As I realize with a start,
it's D-Day at college,
our fest is on,
and the crowds are coming through.

How very forgetful of me!
very important tasks,
lie ahead,
and here I am in bed still waiting for the sun to come up!

So much to do,
run helter-skelter,
after sponsors, after my friends,
pushing and propelling everyone,
to get things done.

Life is hectic,
no time to stand and stare,
if even for a minute,

and only a breath to spare!

Fuming and fretting,
I try to get work going,
rushing to college,
rushing to put up charts,
advertising and tons more!

After a hard day's work,
on my way home,
the train screeches and halts,
And then pushes along,
in the rush of people,
and the sea of faces,
I get pulled and jostled in different directions,
and I can't decide where to turn!
With the rat race getting bigger and dangerous,
A word of caution,
Strive ahead with a strength so new,
That foes lie in fear and your friends grow in numbers!

2. Stormy Mind

Like clouds in a swirl,
Like the strong gusty wind,
Like the swaying of the trees,
Like the stampede of the animals,
Thoughts clog my mind,
And pervade my soul.

There is a whirlwind in my heart,
A storminess in my head,
As I drift far away,
Into my world of dreams,
That's set apart from this world,
Without its mundane problems.

My soul is bare,
full and bursting to its extremes,
it wants to express a thousand many words,
Feelings and emotions,
but fate demands it to be quiet,
And only to listen to others!

I am unable to bear the torture,
the pain.
Oh! The agony of it all!

But to change my fate
Is not in my hands,
But in the palms of the creator above!

3. The Lady in the Sun

The land was parched,
the leaves dry and rustled in the wind,
the cracks in the earth showed up fine,
the pond was dry,
a stillness all around,
not a cloud in the sky,
not a drop of water anywhere,
footsteps, slow and steady,
the jingling of the anklets,
the merriness of the bangles,
the young woman came trudging along,
her feet were bare and worn ,
yet a look of triumph and bravery
with the sun beating down ,
and all of the land still and quiet,
miles and miles to go,
before a pitcher of water gained,
the dusty storms and the fierce winds,
did nothing to stop her going on...
day turned to noon,
and in the distance a light glowed,
the surface of the pond sparkled ,
the glare in her eyes,
and her gaze looking on..

4. Flashing Thunder

A flash of light,
in this darkening sky,
it's not so bright,
and my mind is high.

the clouds shift to make way,
for a thunderous bolt,
that lights up the air,
and crushes our sight.
It begins to pour,
drowning everything in its way,
the rain lashes at the fields,
and floods my mind!

Soon it will be sunny,
the darkness disappeared,
the clouds retreat,
and the earth will be fragrant again!

5. My Love

When life seems bleak,
and the darkness overcomes you,
when storms rise in your mind,
I'll be there for you.

When the road winds and winds,
and the climb is steep,
when the river surges forward,
I'll be waiting right here for you.

When the sun disappears,
and the stars fail to twinkle,
when the shadows follow you around,
I'll be thinking of you.

When you want some love,
when you're looking to make a friend,
when you want me to be there by your side,
I'll be standing right next to you.

6. My Mother

My mother ...
is like a beacon of light that guides me through the night,
a ray of light slicing through the darkness,
a streak of happiness in my life,
a pillar of strength when I need her to be one,
a shower of rain on dry land,
a healing touch to my injured soul,
a wave of joy and euphoria,
the twinkling star in my life,
the candle of hope,
and the wide ocean of happiness that drowns all my sorrows and pain.

7. Dreaming Big

Three simple words to utter
"Learn to dream," and the mind goes aflutter,
It takes no more than a thought,
no more than a chance at believing in oneself,
but questions surround you, when you are fraught,
and you are by yourself.

What does it take to have a dream;
to aspire to be the best in your team?
Goals in place, days of grueling field work,
options unlimited,
until you go berserk;
to recover from the tedium; yet remain addicted.

Never let go of your cherished aspiration,
for what it may do for you, no one can tell, not even a magician!
Striving for something that you can achieve,
is what makes this world go round,
on and on you carry forward, never should be one to deceive,
to make it happen, with happiness profound!

In this maddening crowd of people,
stand out far above as a steeple,

do what it takes to reach the top;
never bow down, never fear for what is right;
never a thought should come to give up or stop.
Stride onwards into the beacon of light!

8. The Stranger in the Mirror

Her eyes are a deadly black,

hair wavy and smooth,

cheeks rosy and soft,

there is a twinkle in her eyes,

a laugh that's perched on her lips,

a shyness that charms you,

a mind that speaks for itself,

a flower that dances in the wind when happy,

and cries when friends are sad,

her love gushes forth ,

and her heart uplifts you when in distress,

who is this stranger in the mirror ,

who keeps staring back at me?

9. Life is Beautiful

Life is beautiful baby,
you just got to see,
in every twinkling star,
in every leaf that rustles in the wind,
in every ripple over the sea,
there is life that calls out to you.

Life is beautiful honey,
Coz no matter who you are,
a second chance always awaits you,
no matter what wrong you do,
there is always time to learn.

Life is beautiful baby,
coz life is all about learning and moving ahead,
be patient and be brave,
Life is indeed very beautiful!

10. Keep Going

Keep going my friend,
down the river of life,
whether there are obstacles,
or even if the sun beats down upon you.

Keep going my friend,
Coz' Life won't give you a second chance,
be strong and brave,
and forge ahead pushing your troubles away.

Keep going my friend,
while it's still calm,
surge through the darkness,
and until night comes.

Keep going my friend,
no matter how difficult the journey,
remember your loved ones,
and make it through.

Keep going my friend,
coz' I'll always be there for you,
through the storms and sorrows,
I'll be right here, waiting for you!

11. The Rain

A drop of the ocean so wide
cools the steaming earth,
as it comes down as a drizzle,
and then a torrent.

It washes away the pain and sorrow,
it refreshes the parched earth,
the trees are immersed in a sprightly dance,
as the water gushes below.
The clouds fill up the sky,
dark, angry and ferocious,
the rain awakens the dead earth,
and makes the flowers smile!

It beats down hard and fearless,
crushing everything beneath,
the plants and their leaves,
and drowns lives!

The rain is welcomed joyfully,
mixed with fear and trepidation,
as the lightning strikes,
and the thunder rolls on..................

12. Happiness

the joy of laughter,
the twinkle of an eye,
the fragrance of flowers,
and the radiance of a smile,
the ripples on the lake,
the chirping of the birds,
the rustle of the leaves with the wind,
the sparkle of a gem,
the shine of an antique,
the gentle touch of softness,
the dancing of feet,
and the sprightly walk,
are happiness put together!

13. Heaven Descends on Earth

The sun shone brightly in the sky,
When over the mountain peaks,
The clouds soared above,
Veiling the sun as they went by.

The sky grew dark,
It turned a melancholy grey,
The birds took flight,
The trees stood morose amidst the vast wilderness.

An eerie stillness prevailed,
Concealing the seething storm under,
The dry river awaited with eagerness the downpour,
While the frightened creatures took refuge.

It began with a drizzle,
Then a little pitter-patter,
Then finally a torrent,
Descending in wild fury.

The river quenched its thirst,
The hidden creatures peered out in wonder,

They brightened up, standing as tall as ever,
For heaven had descended on earth!

14. Solitude

As the sun dips below the horizon,
When one can hear the music playing in the distance,
When the birds fly away home,
And when all the world seems at peace,
Here I sit, accompanied by my solitude.

In a world, in this mad quest for wealth,
Relationships fade away,
Money, money is all that we cry for,
Sleep escapes us,
And greed takes it all away.

All the pains, sorrows surface,
Sinking us further into the quagmire of our own pitfalls,
Nothing seems to please,
Or to quench our thirst,
For true happiness.

Life seems so fruitless,
With no one to be happy
Oh! Lord please redeem us from all this evil,
From greed and filth,
Sin and sacrifices.

Uplift us,
Let this maniacal wildness be shattered
By excitement and love,
Enlighten us oh lord!
And bestow your blessings on us!

15. Heartbreak

A friend who's close,
& who loves you the most,
deserts you now,
and forever more.

To forget and to forgive,
Is hard for me and for you,
So please help me,
To love you forever more.

Friends are forever,
Love stays all along,
So be brave and face,
the blizzards of tomorrow.

My heart is breaking,
Oh! What can I do?
Be my friend,
Be my love.

I'll always be there,
If you need me,

So don't fret,
If you can't get me now!

16. Boundaries

With open arms and a soulful mood,
with hopes on a high,
and dreams galore,
I stride out with a certain nimbleness to take on the world,
leaving far behind old memories and boundaries,
pain and grief,
shadow and darkness,
to emerge like a butterfly from a cocoon,
to spread my wings and fly away,
to reach the distant shores,
and conquer new boundaries,
to reach the acme of success,
to be with the one I love,
to smile at the kiss of a drop of rain,
to bask in the rays of the shining sun,
to cross all boundaries,
and be happy for eternity!

17. Technology: A Boon or a Bane?

As bombshells explode all round,
scarring lives beyond rescue,
smoke clouds the otherwise sunshine-filled house,
the marching of soldiers,
with rifles and AK-47's hoisted up,
the fate of a country ravaged by war seems at stake,
the ammunition and artillery,
the missiles and the rockets,
all seem to pride over a country's defeat!
Lives fall apart and into graves dug deeper and deeper,
there seems no end to this slaughter,
oh lord! have mercy on these poor souls,
who know not what they do.
A missile loses its path and hits an unfortunate target,
another home destroyed and another life lost!
the leaders of our modern hi-tech world may rejoice,
may strike new deals,
but who?
may I ask who?
is even touched by,
the sight of a child crying in pain?
a mother who has lost her son?

a girl who has lost a limb?
a soldier who has lost his will to live?
a country which is left torn and shattered?
a life that has been ripped apart by technological forces?
I repeat ……Are you?

18. The Fruit Basket

With a spring in her step,

and lightness in her heart,

she set out to buy a gift,

for someone so dear,

who'd stand by her through thick and thin,

a little something to keep the memories going,

under the azure sky,

with a gentle breeze blowing,

the glorious day beckoned her,

with a few nickels in hand,

but hopes anew,

the idea of a purchase thrilled her,

the shop seemed far and distant,

filled with gifts and goodies,

each for an occasion,

a nickel here,

or a dime there,

was all there for her to see,

with a look of surprise and cheer,

he welcomed her into the store,

helping her find the perfect gift,

a friend to her since she'd been a baby,

trinkets of varied designs,

and a powder box encrusted with gems of different colors,

it all gleamed under the brightness in the shop,
finally her eyes set upon,
a cute, little basket,
that had pretty pink and white flowers on it,
the handle decorated with ceramic fruits,
"a fruit-basket that is…only ten nickels for you"
I'll take it,
to please my mother,
a birthday gift for her,
to put a smile upon her face!

19. Crepes

As the batter is poured onto the sizzling pan,
a flash of the hand,
and the whirl of the spatula,
with a sprinkling of cinnamon,
as the batter cooks,
It becomes crisp and light,
the chocolate mousse whipped in cream is spread,
nuts of different sizes,
used to garnish,
the chocolate syrup comes next,
winding its way through the cream,
to appear like a brown river of sweetness,
then with a twirl of the hand,
the crispy pancake is wound,
till it forms a cone,
once done, the crepe is ready to eat!

20. The Happenings of a Lazy Sunday!

Rise up and shine,
look out the window and wake up to a day so fine,
The sun peeping behind the clouds,
no need to face the crowds,
the feeling is right,
just so you know i'm upbeat and alright!

Push off the covers,
the pillow with its feathers,
the daylight streaming in,
without the creation of usual din,
a cup of coffee in hand,
staring out the windows to a morning so grand!

Done with breakfast,
now to spend the day in rest,
a book in hand,
coffee cup on the stand,
spectacles ready,
to read something nice and heady!

the morning stretches into noon,
let sleep come over soon,
a scrumptious lunch awaits,
out come the bowls and plates,
another meal devoured,
the mind now dull and blurred!

a lazy Sunday gone by,
I can but not deny,
that the day so wastefully spent,
has some purpose lent,
in refreshing the mind,
facing the Monday ahead leaving Sunday behind!

21. The Journey

An 8:40 train to catch,
just enough time to put on some clothes that don't mismatch,
breakfast in a hurry,
my mind is in a flurry,
so much for this piece of creativity,
that appears to be proclivity.

Scamper into the train station,
wait amidst the crowds for a duration,
when the train screeches to a halt,
there is a sudden rush of people by default,
seats taken, and mind now at peace,
body unscathed and clothes without a crease!

A journey so long,
to a place where I don't belong,
my brain now a bit in a tizzy,
I try to make myself busy,
stations whiz past,
I can't bring myself to keep awake; everything seems so fast!

On and on the train speeds on,

just time to slip on;
my jacket and button it up,
questioned by a fellow passenger, "Are you getting off?", "yup",
the train halts; a force pushes me forward,
the platform kisses my feet and I move, destination in sight, on toward!

About The Author

Kritika Kulshrestha is a corporate communications leader with over 12 years of experience across content marketing, journalism, tech consulting, public relations and corporate communications. A Mumbai gal at heart, Kritika aspires to see the world every single day. With food and travel being her two loves, she feels blessed to have lived and worked in multicultural and multigenerational environments in India, Bahrain and the U.S. and travelled extensively across Europe and Southeast Asia.

In her former role as a journalist, she's interviewed startup founders to CXOs to artists to musicians to opera singers to Off-Broadway performers. Her bylines have appeared in Youth Ki Awaaz, The Daily Texan, Austin Business Journal, Longhorn Life, Austin Fusion Magazine, Cornell Chronicle, Youth Leader Magazine, and Street Authority. Her other stints have included Kroll (formerly Duff & Phelps), Deloitte Consulting, Pixie

Dust Writing Studio, Cornell University, Zirca Digital Solutions, Mad Street Den, Firstpost and Network18, 2 Market Media, Susan Solovic – The Small Business Expert, and Scatter Content.

She's the author of two children's ebooks: "Gifted Kyra" and "Finding the One is Like a Treasure Hunt" published on the Tale Weavers website. She's been a guest on two podcasts: GladiatriX and The First Times.

Kritika was named Communicator of the Year (Marcomm) at exchange4media's 2021 Women Achievers Awards. She was also winner at exchange4media's PR & Corp Comm 40 under 40 Awards 2021. In 2020, she was named a finalist in the Luminary WICA for Growth category at Women's Web's Women in Corporate Allies (WICA) conference. She's been featured in Women's Web magazine and CANDY Magazine, a digital lifestyle publication. She has additionally won awards for her work at Kroll.

She's also founder and circle leader of Lean In Marketing Minds, a community of 50+ women in the fields of marketing, communications, and advertising. She is also VP - Events and Digital Media at the Cornell Club of Mumbai.

Connect with Kritika:

- LinkedIn: https://www.linkedin.com/in/kritikakulshrestha/
- Newsletter: kritikawrites.substack.com

www.ingramcontent.com/pod-product-compliance
Lightning Source LLC
Chambersburg PA
CBHW022124150726
47990CB00003B/1501